Learning to Read, Step by Step!

Ready to Read   Preschool–Kindergarten
• big type and easy words • rhyme and rhythm • picture clues
For children who know the alphabet and are eager to begin reading.

Reading with Help   Preschool–Grade 1
• basic vocabulary • short sentences • simple stories
For children who recognize familiar words and sound out new words with help.

Reading on Your Own   Grades 1–3
• engaging characters • easy-to-follow plots • popular topics
For children who are ready to read on their own.

Reading Paragraphs   Grades 2–3
• challenging vocabulary • short paragraphs • exciting stories
For newly independent readers who read simple sentences with confidence.

Ready for Chapters   Grades 2–4
• chapters • longer paragraphs • full-color art
For children who want to take the plunge into chapter books but still like colorful pictures.

STEP INTO READING® is designed to give every child a successful reading experience. The grade levels are only guides; children will progress through the steps at their own speed, developing confidence in their reading. The F&P Text Level on the back cover serves as another tool to help you choose the right book for your child.

Remember, a lifetime love of reading starts with a single step!

For Tara, an adventurer —S.H.

Text copyright © 2001 by Joyce Milton
Cover art and interior illustrations copyright © 2001 by Shelly Hehenberger

All rights reserved. Published in the United States by Random House Children's Books, a division of Penguin Random House LLC, New York.

Step into Reading, Random House, and the Random House colophon are registered trademarks of Penguin Random House LLC.

Visit us on the Web!
StepIntoReading.com
rhcbooks.com

Educators and librarians, for a variety of teaching tools, visit us at
RHTeachersLibrarians.com

Library of Congress Cataloging-in-Publication Data is available upon request.
ISBN 978-0-593-43274-7 (trade) — ISBN 978-0-593-43275-4 (lib. bdg.)

Printed in the United States of America
10 9 8 7 6 5 4 3 2 1

This book has been officially leveled by using the F&P Text Level Gradient™ Leveling System.

SACAJAWEA
HER TRUE STORY

by Joyce Milton

illustrated by Shelly Hehenberger

Random House 🏠 New York

This is the true story of a young American Indian girl. She lived 200 years ago. Her name was Sacajawea (say: Sah-kah-juh-WEE-ah).

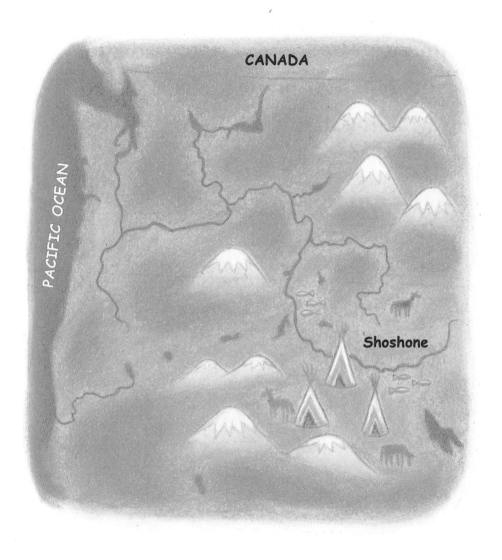

Sacajawea was a Shoshone (say: Show-SHOW-nee) Indian. The Shoshones lived in the Northwest.

The Shoshones loved horses. They used bows and arrows to hunt. Other tribes had guns.

From time to time, other Indians came and stole their horses.

One day, Sacajawea was picking
berries. Suddenly she heard gunfire. It
was a raid! Sacajawea took off across the
river. But she did not get far. A warrior
grabbed her and carried her off.

Sacajawea grew up as a captive of the enemy chief. A fur trader came into camp one day. His name was Charbonneau (say: Shar-bon-OH). He and the chief gambled. When the game was over, the trader had won Sacajawea. She was still a teenager. But now she was the trader's wife.

The trader and his young wife made their way to North Dakota. One day, American explorers appeared on the river. They came in a big barge and two small boats. The Americans had even brought along their pet dog, Seaman. Curious Indians lined the banks to watch.

President Thomas Jefferson had asked the explorers to find a route from the Missouri River to the Pacific Ocean. Their group was led by two men. One was named Meriwether Lewis. The other was Captain William Clark. The Indians called Clark "the red-headed chief."

MERIWETHER LEWIS

WILLIAM CLARK

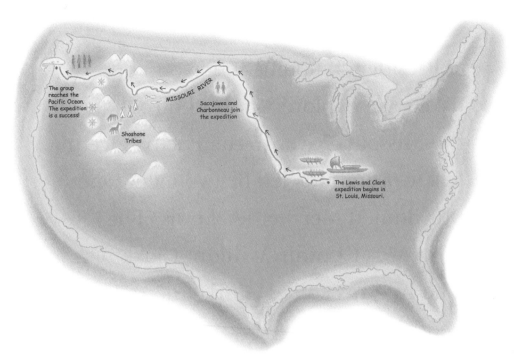

The group
reaches the
Pacific Ocean.
The expedition
is a success!

MISSOURI RIVER

Sacajawea and
Charbonneau join
the expedition

Shoshone
Tribes

The Lewis and Clark
expedition begins in
St. Louis, Missouri.

Sacajawea's husband knew how to talk to the Indians in words and sign language. Lewis and Clark asked him to join their group.

Ice was forming on the river. The explorers built a log fort and waited for the spring.

In the evenings, one of the men would play his violin. The others would dance.

Sacajawea just sat and watched. The white man's music sounded strange to her. She didn't feel like dancing, anyway. She was going to have a baby very soon.

One day in February, Sacajawea felt the baby coming. The pain went on for many hours. Finally, Lewis gave her some medicine. He made it himself, from the tail of a dead rattlesnake. Ten minutes later, Sacajawea had a son. She called him Pomp.

By April, the ice had melted. The explorers were ready to set out with their boats and canoes. The Indians had told Lewis and Clark that mountains lay ahead of them. To get across, they would need horses—Shoshone horses.

Only Sacajawea spoke Shoshone. So she went along with the explorers, with little Pomp on her back.

Right from the start, Sacajawea showed her courage.

One time, a gust of wind tipped her boat. Charbonneau panicked. He dropped the rudder. Boxes of supplies slid into the water.

Sacajawea leaned over the side and grabbed the boxes before they were swept away. Without her quick thinking, the explorers would have been in big trouble!

Soon the group came to a stretch of
rapids and waterfalls. To go any farther,
they would have to load their boats onto
wooden sleds and drag them around
the falls.

The job took many weeks.

Captain Clark and Charbonneau went on ahead to scout the route. They took Sacajawea with them. Even with Pomp on her back, she could walk as fast as the men.

One morning, they were exploring a deep ravine. It started to rain. So everyone huddled under a rock ledge.

Suddenly, Sacajawea heard a loud roar. A wall of water and mud was bearing down on them. It was a flash flood!

Everyone scrambled for high ground. Sacajawea had Pomp in her arms. She couldn't climb very fast. Charbonneau pulled her after him. Captain Clark pushed from behind. They got out of the ravine just in time.

The explorers pushed on. The wide river was now a small stream.

One day, Sacajawea saw a tall rock. She knew this place! The Shoshones called it "Beaver's Head." Their summer hunting grounds must be nearby.

Lewis and a few scouts went ahead. Soon they met three Shoshone women. The women were scared. Were the strangers going to hurt them? But Lewis put red paint on their cheeks. This was a sign of peace. How did he know that? Sacajawea had told him.

The Shoshone chief and some of the Indians went to the explorers' camp. The chief met with Lewis and Clark inside a big tent.

When Sacajawea went inside the tent, her heart filled with joy. The chief was her brother! She burst into tears and rushed to his side.

The chief agreed to sell them horses. Now the explorers could get across the great Rocky Mountains.

It was only September, but the mountain trails were icy. The horses carried the supplies. The men had to walk. Their feet grew numb from the cold.

For once, Sacajawea had an easier
time. She and Pomp got to ride.

There wasn't much food left.
Sacajawea dug up some roots that were
good to eat. But it was not enough for
the hungry men.

Day after day, the men went hunting and returned empty-handed.

Once, they were so hungry that they killed a horse and cooked it. Sacajawea was hungry, too. But she would not eat horse meat.

At last, the highest mountains were behind them. The explorers had reached the lands of a tribe called the Nez Perce (say: Nezz Purse). They wore fancy robes with shells and porcupine quills.

On this side of the mountains the rivers ran west toward the Pacific Ocean.

The explorers set to work building canoes. The Nez Perce agreed to take care of the group's horses.

But now they faced new dangers.

The river was swift and full of rapids.

One canoe hit a rock and flipped over.

Luckily, no one drowned.

Along the banks of the river, there were many Indian villages.

At first, the Indians were ready to attack the strangers. But when they saw Sacajawea and little Pomp, they changed their minds. No war party would bring a mother and baby along.

About 20 miles from the ocean, the explorers made camp for the winter.

One day there was news. A monster had washed up on the beach! Captain Clark knew that the monster must be a whale. He decided to take a few men and get some of the whale meat.

Sacajawea begged to go along. She had come all this way. She wanted to see the great sea. Clark agreed.

On a cold day in January in 1806, Sacajawea got her wish. She looked out over the Pacific Ocean.

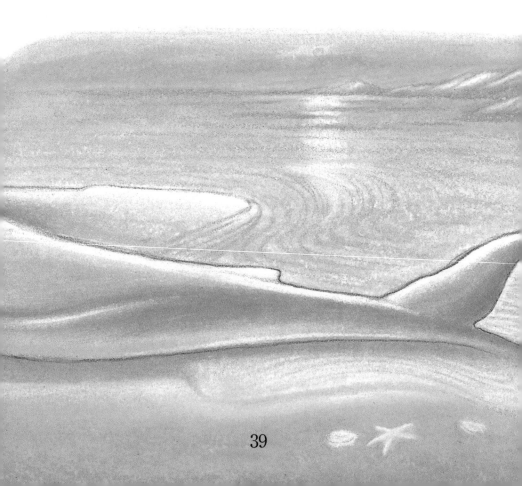

When spring came, the explorers were ready for their return trip.

On the way back, they faced more hardships. But Sacajawea was always cheerful. Captain Clark admired her for that. He gave her the nickname "Janey." He called Pomp "my dancing boy."

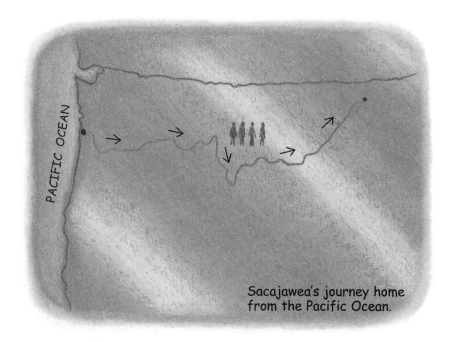

Sacajawea's journey home from the Pacific Ocean.

At one point, Pomp came down with a high fever. Clark tried everything to save him. He even made a cream out of bear fat to rub on the little boy's neck. It worked! Soon Pomp was well again.

At last, the explorers reached their old winter fort in North Dakota. They had been away for one year and four months. The Indians welcomed them with loud cheers and gifts of corn.

Now it was time for Sacajawea to say good-bye to Lewis and Clark. Captain Clark offered to adopt Pomp and send him to school. Sacajawea said no. Pomp was too young to leave her.

Two years later, Charbonneau and his family moved to St. Louis. They bought a little farm from Captain Clark.

But the fur trader couldn't get used to the quiet life of a farmer. He and his wife joined a group of traders headed for the Dakotas.

In the winter of 1812, news came that Charbonneau's young wife had died there of a bad fever.

Was this the end of Sacajawea? Maybe not. The Shoshones say that the woman who died was another wife of Charbonneau. They say Sacajawea had left her husband and had gone to live with the Comanche tribe.

Many years later, an old woman returned to the lands of the Shoshones. She talked about Lewis and Clark's journey to the Pacific. She showed people a medal with President Jefferson's picture on it. Was this woman the real Sacajawea? If so, she lived to be almost 100 years old.

There are still many mysteries about the life of Sacajawea. But we do know that she was strong and full of courage. She was part of a great adventure. Today we honor her with a golden dollar coin.